# CONTENTS

Words printed in **bold letters like these** are explained in the Glossary.

# WHY DO CUTS BLEED?

If you fall and cut yourself, red blood oozes out of the wound. It doesn't matter where the skin is broken, it always bleeds. This is because your skin is criss-crossed by tiny tubes that carry blood. The tubes are so narrow you can see them only under a microscope. But you can see the blood that leaks out when some of them are damaged.

## Keeping dirt out

It is important not to let dirt and germs get into your body through the wound. Bleeding washes dirt and germs out of the cut and so helps to protect the body. Make sure a cut is clean and cover it with a plaster. Rubbing a little antiseptic cream on the inside of the plaster also helps to kill germs.

This girl has fallen off her bicycle and cut her arm.

## Does bleeding matter?

It might look alarming to see blood trickling from a cut, but don't worry. Older children have about 4 litres of blood altogether, so your body will not miss a little bit. If the cut is very deep and blood is pouring out, then it is important to get help fast to stop the bleeding.

## DON'T TOUCH SOMEONE ELSE'S BLOOD

Blood can carry germs, so it is important not to let other people's blood inside your body. Always use kitchen roll or a clean cloth to clean someone else's cut.

This photograph has been magnified so that you can see the tiny tubes that carry blood through the skin.

## Capillaries

The tiny tubes that carry blood through your skin are called **capillaries**. There are capillaries in every part of your body, including your bones and muscles and all the **organs**, such as your liver, heart, stomach and brain. Only your hair and nails are not filled with blood. There is blood under your nails but not in the nails themselves. This is why they do not bleed when you cut them.

## Arteries

Capillaries are part of a one-way system of tubes that carries blood from the heart around the body and back to the heart. The heart pushes blood into large tubes called **arteries**. One artery goes from the heart to the lungs. The largest artery is 2.5 centimetres wide and takes blood from the heart to the rest of the body. It branches into narrower arteries: one for each arm, two to your head and one to your lower body. Each artery branches into narrower and narrower arteries and then into capillaries.

The heart pumps blood through the arteries (shown in orange-red). It returns to the heart through the veins (shown in purple-red).

heart

Veins

Arteries

## Veins

When the blood has reached the furthest capillaries, it begins to travel back to the heart. The capillaries join together into wider tubes that lead into the **veins**. You can see some of the veins that carry blood back to your heart on the inside of the wrist. The veins join up and take the blood into the heart.

## A NETWORK OF TUBES

Tubes that carry blood are called **blood vessels** and you have about 96,000 km of them. Most are capillaries. If all your blood vessels were laid out end to end, they would stretch twice around the world.

Capillaries link the arteries to the veins. Blood travels through the capillaries in each part of the body and then into the veins.

artery

network of capillaries

vein

# WHY DO CUTS FORM SCABS?

Scabs are the body's way of protecting an open wound while the skin below it heals. When the skin is damaged and broken, it bleeds. As blood flows through the wound, it becomes thicker and starts to clot.

## Sticky blood cells

Blood contains special **cells** called **platelets**. They stick together to form a plug in the walls of the damaged **capillaries**. Other chemicals in the blood form a web of strands across the wound. Platelets become trapped in the web and form a large clot of blood mixed with other cells. This dries to form a hard scab that keeps out dirt and germs.

When you damage your skin, the wound heals by forming a scab.

How a wound heals

1 A clot of blood forms over the wound and stops it bleeding.

2 The clot hardens and shrinks to form a scab.

3 New skin grows below the scab.

## New skin

The body is very good at repairing itself. The walls of the capillaries that were torn or cut are soon replaced. New skin slowly grows across the wound. At the same time, the scab dries out and begins to shrink. When it falls off you can see the new, pink skin underneath. Do not pick at a scab before it is ready to fall off. If you do, the wound below may open up and start to bleed again.

## Large wounds

A large wound or deep cut may have to be stitched to help it heal. Only a nurse or doctor should do this. The stitches hold the edges of the wound together while it heals. Wounds that are stitched do not form scabs, but they may leave a scar. Scars slowly fade, but can last for years.

This wound has been stitched to help it heal better. These stitches will be removed later.

# WHY DO BRUISES CHANGE COLOUR?

A bruise is caused by bleeding below the skin. The blood spilt below the skin slowly breaks down and is absorbed by fresh blood. As this happens, the bruise changes colour – from blue-black to purple to yellow.

## What causes a bruise?

Underneath your skin are layers of fat and muscle covering your bones and **organs**, such as your stomach and liver. If something sharp hits the skin, it cuts through it and you bleed. But if something blunt hits the skin, the force of the blow is spread out over a large area. The skin is not broken but some of the tiny **capillaries** in the skin and flesh below may be damaged so that blood leaks from the capillaries into the flesh around.

This boy fell downstairs and has a huge bruise on his shin. The bruise is blue-black to begin with, but changes to yellow as it slowly disappears.

bruise

## Swelling

When any part of the body is damaged, extra blood floods into the area. The blood helps to repair the damage. The extra blood makes the skin go red and can make the flesh swell. The swelling forms a cushion around the damaged area and protects it from further damage. If you fall and knock your head, for example, a lump might quickly form on your scalp or forehead.

## How a bruise heals

When the **cells** of the spilt blood die, they turn blue-black. It can take a few hours for a bruise to show below the skin. But it takes many days for fresh blood to destroy and remove all the dead cells.

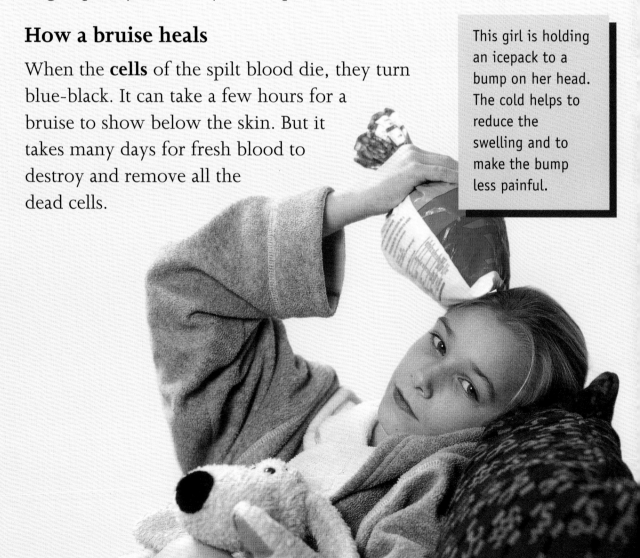

This girl is holding an icepack to a bump on her head. The cold helps to reduce the swelling and to make the bump less painful.

# WHY IS BLOOD RED?

Blood contains three main kinds of cells – red cells, white cells and platelets.

Blood is made of a watery liquid called **plasma** with billions of tiny blood **cells** floating in it. The three main kinds of blood cells are red cells, white cells and **platelets**. Blood is red because there are many more red cells than any other kind of cell.

Platelets

Plasma

## Red cells

The red substance in red blood cells is called **haemoglobin**. The main job of red blood cells is to carry oxygen from your lungs to all the cells in your body. The oxygen sticks to the haemoglobin and turns it bright red. When the haemoglobin lets go of its oxygen, it becomes dull red.

## White cells and platelets

White blood cells kill germs that get inside your body and also remove dead cells. White cells are larger than other blood cells. They surround

White blood cells

Red blood cells

the germ or dead cell and destroy it. Platelets are small cells that help your blood to clot when you cut yourself.

## Short life

Each red blood cell lives only for about four months, so your body has to constantly make new cells to replace them. It makes about two million new red blood cells every second! New red blood cells are made in the **marrow**, the soft jelly-like substance in the middle of some bones. Some white cells, however, can live for many years.

## MILLIONS OF RED CELLS

A tiny drop of blood no bigger than the head of a pin contains 9000 white cells, 250,000 platelets and 5,000,000 red cells. An adult has about 5 litres of blood. This means they have 25 million million red cells.

Blood cells are too small to see except through a microscope. This person is looking at a sample of blood to see whether it is healthy.

## Many kinds of cells

Every part of the body is made up of tiny **cells**. Your skin is made of skin cells, your bones of bone cells, and so on. Every living cell needs food and oxygen to keep it alive.

## A transport system

Blood is a kind of transport system. It delivers food and oxygen to every cell and takes away waste. The food you eat is broken down in your stomach and **intestines** and the useful parts pass into the blood. It is taken to your liver and stored. The liver keeps your blood stocked with a good supply of glucose, the substance your cells burn to get the energy they need to do their job.

You need to eat food to stay alive. When the food has been processed by the digestive system, it is carried in the blood to every part of the body.

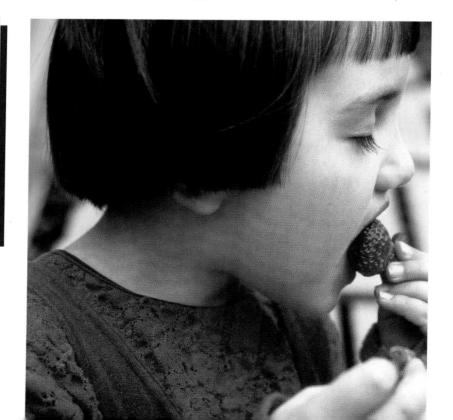

## Taking away waste

As a cell uses glucose it produces heat and the gas carbon dioxide. This waste gas is carried in the blood back to the lungs. Here it leaves the blood and joins the air that you breathe out.

## Other things carried in the blood

The blood carries many things apart from food and oxygen around the body. If you take a pill to cure a headache, for example, the chemicals in the pill are carried around your body in your blood. When they reach your head, they help it stop the ache. Alcohol and other poisons pass into the blood too. The liver destroys poisons but it can only deal with small amounts at a time. Alcohol in the blood affects many parts of the body including the brain.

The blood supplies each cell with food and oxygen. It carries away waste carbon dioxide.

cell

blood

| Key | | |
|---|---|---|
| oxygen ➡ | carbon dioxide ➡ | particles of food ➡ |

# WHY DO MY FEET GET COLD FIRST?

The body makes most of its own heat by burning food. The temperature of most of your body is normally 37° Celsius. Blood carries heat from the centre of the body to your hands and feet, but it loses some of its heat on the way. Since blood has to travel furthest to reach your feet and toes, they are usually the first to become cold. Your fingers may also feel cold, because blood has to travel a long way to reach them too.

Wearing warm socks and slippers help to stop your feet losing heat.

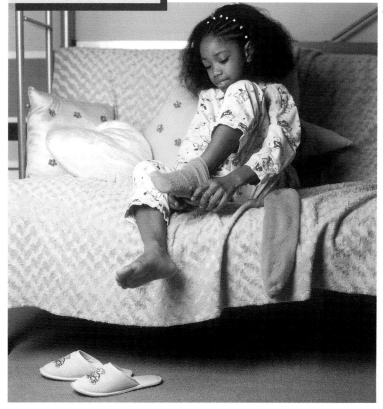

## Losing heat

Most heat is lost from your body through the tiny **capillaries** in your skin. When you are in a cold place, the capillaries become narrower. This means that less blood comes to the surface of your body and so less heat is lost. But it also means that your toes and fingers get less warm blood and feel even colder!

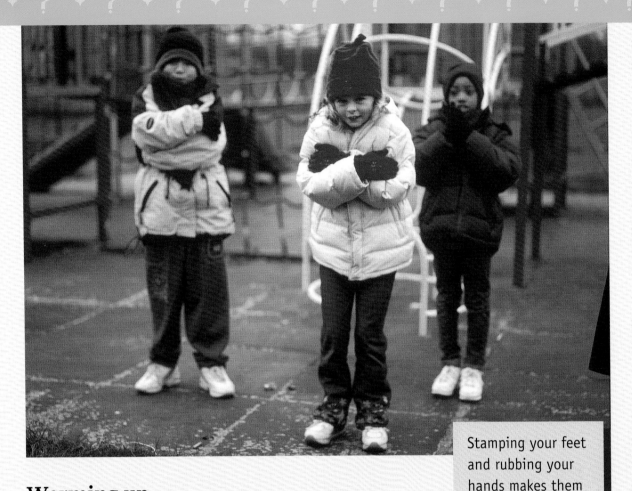

## Warming up

When you are cold, a good way to warm up is to move around and exercise your muscles. Muscles make heat as they work. The blood takes in this heat and carries it around your body. The harder you exercise, the faster your heart beats. This pushes the warm blood around your body faster.

Stamping your feet and rubbing your hands makes them warmer. It brings more warm blood into your fingers and toes.

## Cooling down

Blood also helps to cool you down when you are hot. The capillaries in your skin become wider. This makes your skin red and hot but it allows some of the heat to escape from the body.

17

# WHAT DOES MY HEART DO?

Your heart is more or less in the centre of your chest between your lungs and behind your breastbone. If you place your hand here, you may feel your heart beating.

The heart pumps blood to the lungs and around the body. First, blood leaves the heart and goes to the lungs. Here it takes in oxygen before returning to the heart. The heart then pumps blood that is rich with oxygen around the body.

## What does my heart look like?

Your heart does not look very romantic. It is a slimy, throbbing **organ** that fills and spurts with blood. The heart is made of a special kind of muscle which is very strong. Muscles work by contracting, that is by getting smaller. When the heart contracts, it squeezes blood into the **arteries**. The force it produces is about the same as it takes to squeeze a tennis ball.

## How big is my heart?

Curl your fingers into the palm of your hand to make a fist.

18

This is how big your heart is. The bigger you are, the bigger your heart is, but the bigger your fist is too, so an adult's heart is also about the same size as their fist.

## Circulation

Blood circulates around the body, but each drop of blood does not go to every part of the body. Instead the arteries, **capillaries** and **veins** form several separate systems. For example, some blood goes to the head and back to the heart. A large artery takes blood to the lower body but it branches into several main arteries. Each of these arteries has its own circulation system.

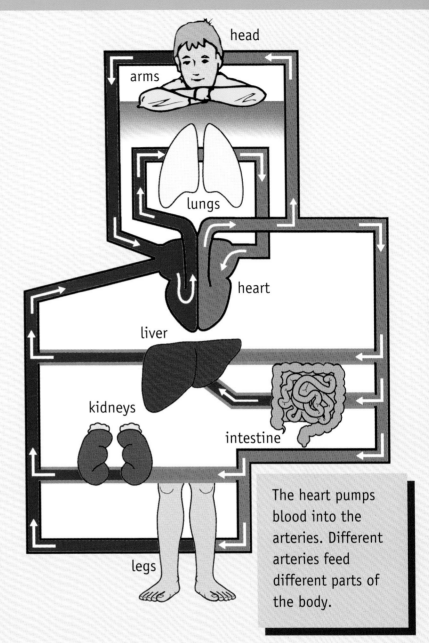

head

arms

lungs

heart

liver

kidneys

intestine

legs

The heart pumps blood into the arteries. Different arteries feed different parts of the body.

## CONSTANT CIRCULATION

Blood travels round the body nearly 2000 times a day. So every drop of blood passes through the heart about once a minute.

## Inside the heart

A heart is divided into two halves. Each half has two spaces or chambers. This is because the heart is not one pump, but two pumps that work together. The chambers on the right side pump blood to the lungs. Those on the left side pump blood to the body. The left side is slightly larger than the right because it has a bigger job to do.

## Journey through the heart

Blood from the body is brought into the upper right chamber and flows into the larger, lower chamber. As the heart contracts, the blood is pushed through the **artery** to the lungs. There it picks up oxygen and returns to the left side of the heart. It flows from the upper into the lower left chamber. From there it is squeezed into the artery that takes it to the body.

## Valves

The heart has four **valves** that control the flow of blood and make it flow only in the right direction. Valves between the upper and lower chambers open to allow blood to flow into the lower chambers. They close as the heart contracts. At the same time valves between the lower chambers and the arteries open. Now the only way the blood can go is out of the heart and into the arteries.

### TIRELESS HEART

The heart never rests. It usually beats at least 60 to 70 times a minute. So it beats:
- about 4000 times every hour
- nearly 100,000 times a day
- over 2,500,000,000 times in an average lifetime.

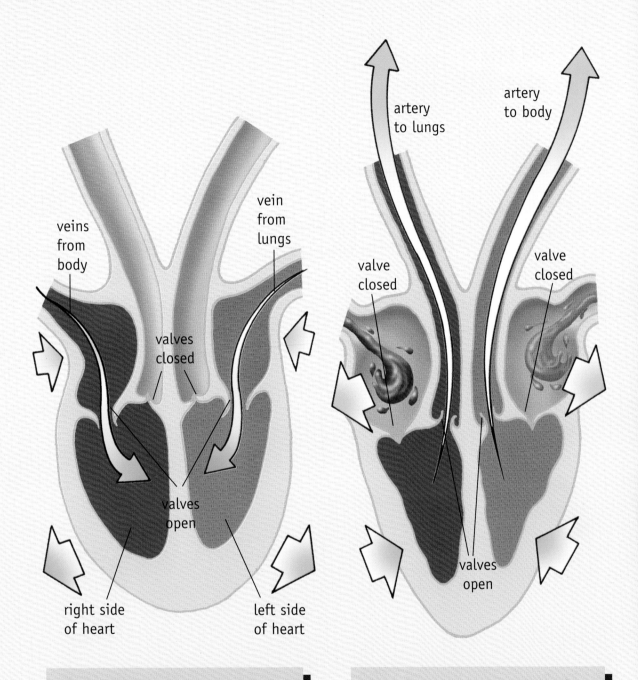

veins
from
body

vein
from
lungs

valves
closed

valves
open

right side
of heart

left side
of heart

artery
to lungs

artery
to body

valve
closed

valve
closed

valves
open

Valves between the upper and lower chambers open to allow blood from the **veins** to flow in.

As the heart contracts, the valves from the upper chambers close and those to the arteries open to force the blood through them.

# WHAT KEEPS MY HEART BEATING?

A group of **cells** in the right upper chamber controls your heart-beat. These cells are the heart's **pacemaker**. They produce a wave of electrical signals that spreads through the heart muscle and makes it contract.

## ECG

Doctors use a machine called an electrocardiograph (ECG) to check whether a patient's heart is beating properly. **Electrodes** are placed on the patient's chest. They pick up the heart's electrical signals and the machine displays them on a screen, or it can print them out.

The ECG machine records the electrical signals that make the heart beat. They show as blips on the screen.

## Measuring heart-beat

You can measure your own heart-beat by taking your **pulse**. If you place your fingers over your wrist as shown below, you will feel a regular throb. Every time the heart beats it causes a wave of blood to spurt through the **arteries**. It is the spurt of blood that you feel as a pulse.

## ARTIFICIAL PACEMAKER

Sometimes the heart's pacemaker stops working properly. Then doctors fit an artificial pacemaker just below the skin. It is powered by batteries and sends a regular signal to the heart to tell it to beat.

## Stethoscope

Doctors use a stethoscope to listen to your heart beat. It magnifies the sound so that they can hear your heart working. What they hear is not a single beat, but a 'lub-dup' – the sound of the **valves** slamming shut. The 'lub' is made by the valves between the upper and lower chambers closing. The 'dup' is the sound of the valves to the arteries closing.

This boy is measuring his own pulse. He counts how many beats he can feel in a minute.

# WHAT MAKES MY HEART BEAT FASTER?

Many things can make your heart beat faster, including exercise, fear and some drugs.

## Exercise

Muscles take oxygen and food from the blood to give them the energy they need to work. When you exercise, your muscles work hard and so use more oxygen and food. You gulp in extra air and your heart beats faster to supply the muscles with oxygen and food. Exercise strengthens your muscles and makes them work better. This includes the muscles in your heart.

Running makes your heart work faster and better, so that it supplies your muscles and brain with extra oxygen.

## Fear

If you feel scared or anxious, your heart may beat faster. If a snarling dog suddenly jumps at you, your heart may begin to pound. Your body speeds up your heart-beat and sends extra blood to your brain and muscles. You become more alert and your muscles tense, ready for action.

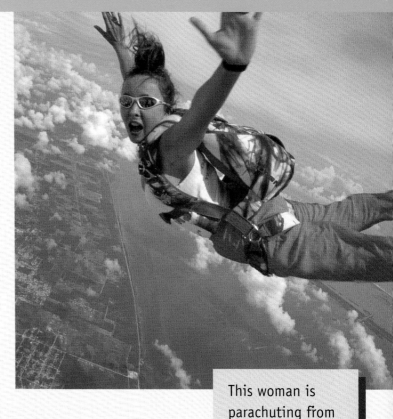

This woman is parachuting from a plane for the first time. Her heart is probably pounding!

## Drugs

Caffeine in tea, coffee and cola is a drug that makes your heart beat faster. You probably won't notice that it has speeded up, but you will feel more alert. Some drugs make the heart beat dangerously fast. People who sniff aerosols, for example, are more likely to suffer from a heart attack.

## FAST DELIVERY

Normally your heart pumps about 5 litres of blood a minute around the body. Exercise makes it beat faster, pumping up to 25 litres of blood a minute.

# WHAT CAUSES A HEART ATTACK?

A heart attack occurs when part of the heart muscle stops working. The heart has its own **arteries** that supply it with blood. If one of these arteries becomes blocked, the muscle is starved of oxygen and stops working.

## Blocked arteries

A person suffers from heart disease when the arteries that supply the heart become furred up and narrower. The heart has to work harder to push blood through them. Heart disease can cause pain and so the problem is often diagnosed before a heart attack occurs. A surgeon can sometimes unblock the arteries and make them wider again. If this operation does not work, the patient may have a heart by-pass operation, in which the damaged arteries are replaced by healthy **blood vessels**.

A surgeon is pushing a narrow instrument through the arteries of the patient's heart. It will unblock the arteries to make the heart healthier.

## A healthy life

Heart disease is one of the commonest causes of death among people who are over the age of 50. The best way to avoid heart disease when you are older is to live a healthy life when you are young. There are four things you can do to keep your heart healthy: don't smoke tobacco, avoid very fatty food, exercise regularly and stay calm.

## Smoking

Smoking tobacco affects the heart in several ways. Carbon monoxide in tobacco smoke takes the place of oxygen in the blood, so that the body, including the heart, is deprived of oxygen. Nicotine in tobacco makes the arteries constrict and become narrower. And, for people who smoke regularly, nicotine contributes to their arteries becoming furred up.

A person who smokes is twice as likely to have a heart attack as a non-smoker.

## Fat and cholesterol

Many fatty foods contain a substance called cholesterol. Cholesterol sticks to the inside of the **arteries** and makes them narrower. People with high cholesterol or who are overweight are more likely to suffer from heart disease. The best way to cut down on cholesterol and lose extra fat is to eat less fatty food and take plenty of exercise.

## Exercise

Taking regular exercise will make your heart work better so that it pumps more blood through your body with every beat and does not have to work so hard. To be fit, you should exercise so that your heart-beat is increased for 20 to 30 minutes at least three times a week.

## Stress

Stress makes your heart beat faster. If this happens for long periods of time, your heart may become strained. Relaxing makes your heart beat slower.

These are some foods that are good for your heart.

# BODY MAP

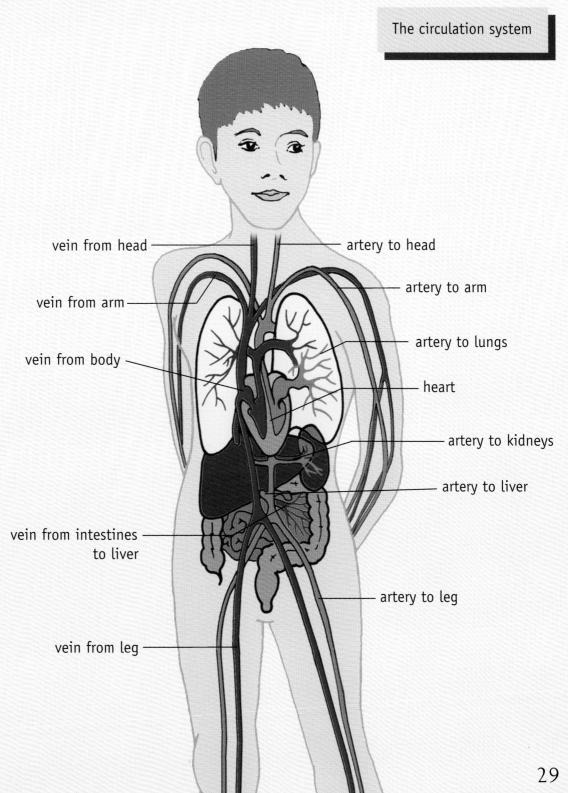

vein from head

artery to head

vein from arm

artery to arm

artery to lungs

vein from body

heart

artery to kidneys

artery to liver

vein from intestines
to liver

artery to leg

vein from leg

# GLOSSARY

**arteries**   blood vessels that carry blood from the heart to other parts of the body

**blood vessels**   tubes that carry blood

**capillaries**   very thin blood vessels that join the ends of the arteries to the veins

**cell**   the smallest building block of living things. The body has many kinds of cells, including different kinds of blood cells, bone cells and skin cells.

**electrode**   a device that conducts electricity

**haemoglobin**   the red substance in red blood cells that joins with oxygen from the lungs and carries it to all the cells in the body

**intestines**   the long tube that food passes into after it leaves the stomach

**marrow**   the soft, jelly-like substance found at the centre of many bones

**organ**   part of the body, for example the heart, that carries out a particular process

**pacemaker**   a group of cells in the heart or an artificial device that sends out signals to make the heart beat regularly

**plasma** the clear liquid that other kinds of blood cells float in

**platelets** a kind of blood cell that makes blood clot and so helps to heal wounds

**pulse** a throb or beat which can be felt at various points of the body. It is caused by a surge of blood as the heart contracts and is used to measure heart-beat.

**valve** a device that controls the flow of a liquid or gas. Valves in the heart open and close to allow blood to flow through the heart. Valves also prevent blood from flowing in the wrong direction.

**veins** blood vessels that carry blood from the capillaries back to the heart

# FURTHER READING

Body Books: Blood red? A Ganeri, 2002, Evans

Body matters: *Why do I sneeze? and other questions about breathing*, A Royston, 2002, Heinemann Library

Body matters: *Why do I vomit? and other questions about digestion*, A Royston, 2002, Heinemann Library

# INDEX